Blarney Poems

– FRANK CONDON –

FASTPRINT PUBLISHING
PETERBOROUGH, ENGLAND

BLARNEY POEMS
Copyright © Frank Condon 2009

All rights reserved.

No part of this book may be reproduced in any form by photocopying or any electronic or mechanical means, including information storage or retrieval systems, without permission in writing from both the copyright owner and the publisher of the book.

ISBN 978-184426-699-9

First published 2009 by
FASTPRINT PUBLISHING
Peterborough, England.

Printed by
www.printondemand-worldwide.com

4th July Baby
Frank Condon

A product of love mother said
This in answer to my childish question
But borne to be born in the heat of summer?
This was surely to neither mother's or baby likes

Oh for a cool spot where warmth could be displaced
This simple sought after source by a child bearing mother
And thereby lay a flat iron gate
Could this yield up coolness to a hot fevered brow?

She had found a spot to her liking
And yet but a tiny part of her heat reddened brow felt its coolness
A coolness from a rust covered surface but welcomed
Only two inches wide and yet it provided for a desperate need

Junior too inside a warm wet womb gave indication that
It too was aware of his mother's actions
And its response to this provider's action
A somersault or something similar

Coolness absorbed move along a need still existed

Another cool steel surface
A white rusty band shows on sweat covered forehead
How silly was the pregnant woman's action?

Never mind. A week later baby Tim was born
An Independence Day 4th July baby
And the hot July weather? It still persisted.

Oh for a Baldy Dog
Frank Condon

The dog wasn't ours, not even on loan
Yet we felt obliged to give it a home.
A hairy thing of coat tan and white
That shed it short hairs both day and night.

Hairs on the furniture but not on the wall
Hairs on the carpet on stairs in our hall.
Hairs on our clothes even on its own rug
Hopefully soon we'll have **a baldy dog?**

If it scratches itself there's a hairy storm
When it shook itself there was cause for alarm.
I have seen hairs on gooseberries and on a hog
But I've never ever seen **a hairless dog?**

Where do hairs come from, can they grow so fast?

With thousands of hairs falling 'twill never last
May be we'll start giving her a pint of grog
Could we then hopefully end up with **a hairless dog**.

I've seen wrinkled hounds, ugly things.
I've seen little dogs going round in rings
But a hairless ape or a multi coloured frog
Hold no comparison I'd Love **a baldy dog.**

A Dinkum Poem.
Frank Condon.

I sat beneath a blue gum tree its stringy bark around, no good to neither man nor beast this bark upon the ground. How sad I thought to see a tree devoid of bark and dying this tree it was a blue gum folks so dry your tears no crying. The blue gum has no need for bark to sustain its way of life it has a pith of fibrous moist to avoid the dry weather strife. This tree it isn't blue at all for blue is a mistake or error, it's the name for a redheaded person or even a busted mirror. Now if crook is sick and Tucker's food and Dinkum means it's true and Bludger is a scrounger, it is I'm telling you.

Now Smoko is a tea break a smoke or break for food and sausages are know as Snags and Bonza means it's good.

Galah it is a stupid person it's also a stupid bird and Spensers and Sreddies are underwear they are upon my word.

Now Dunny's an outside toilet and Durex is sticky tape a Gum tree a Eucalyptus Tree then a Paddock's a field or open space.

A Dream will do

Air: Spansil Hill
Frank Condon.

I awoke last night at midnight; I was sad and all alone.
For I dreamt I was back home again in old New Ross my home,
I crossed the Barrow River on the old bridge I remember it still
And I headed up through Bridge Street on my way to the High Hill.

I stopped beside the Royal hotel to catch some memories
Where looking down through North Street the Tolstel I could see.
I passed by Hanrahan's public house I worked there as a lad
Looking after Jimmy's greyhounds was it four or five he had?

The 'Mile bush Flyer' was one of them I feared would come to harm
When he broke away one stormy day the thunder it did alarm.
Tearing down the Goat hill it gave me a chill, empty collar still in my hand.
'Twas by the pink rock, they found Jimmy's dog, and him sitting on the sand!

Then on past Meagher's bake house where a baker I thought I'd be
From early morn 'till dewey eve I worked almost for free
But Meagher changed his mind after he did find, eating cakes 'till I'd had me fill
Up in Barrack lane where he did complain, but for that I'd be working there still.

The cakes were for sale Mr. Meagher did wail and so I got the sack
The more I'd plead for my family's need he wouldn't have me back.
So I joined the unemployable lads and I'm sure I be there still
By the royal Hotel, stories we would tell, at the foot of the High hill!

Through South Street then I did proceed meeting friends now and then
'Till I stopped awhile and it made me smile, beside the L and N
As a delivery boy I was full of joy, they supplied me with a bike
I loved that job, they only paid a few bob but that was a job that I like.

Until one day when me brakes gave way, down Cross lane I was going fast

Going faster still at the foot of the hill going through O'Brian's showroom glass.
The L and N paid for the glass after that big smash and told me to take a hike
That how I lost my place with a bleeding cut face and they took away their bike.

In Priory Place sure it's a disgrace, they had closed the Tanyard down
I remember well and folks will tell, they missed that hooter's sound
Fond memories it did me please and imagine I remembered it still
By the showground's I stand, with me cap in me hand, at the foot of Jones's hill

A quicksave plastic bag.
Frank Condon.

He left Quicksave, with a friendly wave, and went walking on up the hill.

He walked on until, he reached the hill, hoping someone to meet.

But alas and alac, with an aching back, he was forced to carry on.

With the bags so full, on his shoulders pull, he knew that he'd got it wrong.

No one could save, this poor old slave, who was stuck with shopping alone.

But now no way, any other day, he would choose to stay at home.

With no wife to help, he was stuck on the shelf, treated like an oily old rag

His life would be fare, with some one to share, the contents of his Quicksave plastic bag.

Another show?
Frank Condon.

Well the disappointment's worn off we have started up at last
This time though things will be different we have a smaller cast.
This time our play has only one act last time we had three.
We'll put it on in just six weeks; we will, just wait and see.

Our leading lady's still with us, the fathers still the same.
In fact we've got the same cast we have only changed the name.
A variety act someone had said, as well as a one-act play.
We have gone much further this time, we have gone and named the day.

At first the end of July some one of us this cry
A little later then was said, at least give it a try.

And so we tossed it back and forth, oh please don't let it be late.
The end of august then we choose and they all agreed 'twas great.

We knew 'Twould not be easy for it had not been done before
Would anybody listen could an audience be coaxed through the door.
We couldn't do it for nothing, we would ask the people to pay
And hope they would enjoy themselves when at last we do our play.

We hope that we'll amaze them all with all the things we do
We really have some talent our little drama crew.
Sketches we have in plenty, with every kind of acts
So come one, come all, and fill our hall, then you can judge the facts.

Autumn sadness.
Frank Condon.

The autumn means nothing but the fall of the year
Now there is a word that has meaning that's clear.
For when something is falling it will end on the floor,
Like the leaves that are wind shorn will grow never more.

But before the leaves flutter and fall without sound
They bedazzle us all as they glide towards the ground.
Like tear drops the leaves fall on a bare brown soil
Little pay for tree's labour in spring where lay toil

Their seed lay in kernels like brown coffins of wood
That the squirrels must bury for that's as it should.
For all nature they signal summer's end won't be long
The birds take that signal to add sadness to song.

The days they get shorter adding length to our night
The wind rises and rain clouds hide the sun from our sight

There is nothing here now but decay all abound
As the year cries in sadness that Autumn around.

Autumn 2
Frank Condon.

I remember a time in the fall of the year, when in the U S A.

When Massachusetts and New England nearly took my breath away.

From Boston down to Plymouth Rock and as far as the eye could see,

The colours there were beautiful as nature coloured each tree.

The summer here was fading fast and another season started

But Mother Nature hung in there still from her duty she wouldn't be parted.

The reds, the olive and chestnut, the green the orange and brown,

Abound on every side now in the countryside and town.

Here nature flaunts her colours as she takes a well-earned rest

While putting away her summer clothes, she shows her autumn's best.

For now as days grow shorter, which make the night seem long,

There is just that hint of sorrow in the whippoorwill's even' song.

The greenish hues of summer bright are dappled now and faded

But look what autumn had to show, her colours here paraded.

From New Bedford through Fall River the signs are all around

The signs that autumn's here at last and has her coloured carpet down.

Black Roots of Ballyanne
Frank Condon.

When the black Rooks came to Ballyanne
To the trees very near our gate.
They loudly spoke from branches high
Hoping each spring to attract a mate.

On the first of March, on that very day
Their building started then,
High rise building nests, as they were seen
No permission sought from men.

Reports were sent in daily
As the building boom progressed
Bringing officials from the council
With regulations, as you guessed.

This flight of Rooks year after year
Had built among these trees
What men controlled was nothing to them
Rooks were gone before the leaves.

And round those leafless branches
New generation there were bred.
They never asked for handouts
When their young was daily fed.

But this year things were different
Now the Celtic Tiger days are here.
There are new building regulations
The regulations are very clear.

"Who submitted your building plans?
One shrewd planning officer cried?
Now cease, belay all building work,
You can not build this side."

The shouted words of officialdom,
Quoting regulations very terse.
Did it slow the black Rooks building work?
Did it put it in reverse?

Each day the sun rose higher
Until sun grew hot and strong,
With increased threats of demolition
From the councilman.

The young hatched out and spread their wings
Very soon they would be gone
And still the councilman was there
When the Rooks left Ballyanne.

BREAD AND BUTTER BOYS.
Frank Condon.

I will tell a tale of my boyhood adventures
To the little grandson sitting on me knee
How we headed West just like the cowboys
And all we had was bread and butter for our tea.

If you ever go across the Irish Sea to Ireland
By Ferry, Plane or even under sail.
You will be surprised by all the changes
Whether your Spinster, Widower or Single Male.

For start the ould journey very short now
And for this we should be thankful to our God
You might have spent the night on a cattle boat lad
Or aboard a vessel the named the 'Princess Maude.'

When still a lad I remember well the heartbreak
Of leaving home to settle across the sea
Along with hundreds of other manly hopefuls
Seeking a better way of living just like me.

Me mother packed me case and small brown paper parcel
She lovingly placed into my shaking hand
'It's just a bit of mate and Denny's sausages
You'll enjoy them when you reach that foreign land'.

In an open hold we sat on slatted benches
The stars above below the raging sea
Sure on those crossings everyone was sick lad
And I'd only had bread and butter for me tea!

With empty stomachs we'd dock at morn in Holyhead
With case in hand we'd trudge through blustery gales
Someone of us asked of me 'Are we in England?'
Was disappointed to be told 'We're still in Wales.

On the train we found a little bit of comfort
As the train pulled out 'twas bound for London Town
We found a seat and stowed our battered suitcase
In huddled forms all soaking wet we settled down'

So if you ever cross the Irish Sea to Ireland
Will you be thinking of the guys that crossed like me
When we crossed the Irish Sea behind St. Patrick
And we'd only had bread and butter for our tea.

By the Cemetery Wall.
Frank Condon.

'Twas in that cemetery that I had a scare

When I saw a man but was he there?
I looked away but then looked back
Just for a moment had I seen Jack?

Jack was my brother very young when he died

And all that day I cried and cried.

At what age you die or so they say

You remain forever and a day.

But why had this man I only saw his back

Remind me of my brother Jack?

Was it the way he held his head?

I know, I know Jack's a long time dead.

Was it something he was going to say?
Then changed his mind and walked away
Was it a man that I'd seen at all?
Or just a shadow on the graveyard wall?

Each day I return each day I go back
Hoping that it is my brother Jack.
I have this need to put things right
Twixt my brother and I when we had that fight.

Some day, some day I hope the most
I'll see poor Jack even as a ghost
To tell him I'm sorry, if only if
We hadn't been fighting beside that cliff.

I can still hear his terrified scream
It happened so quickly or was it a dream?
My life's full of torment the future looks black
I'm miserable now without my brother Jack.

With parents now dead that leaves only me
If Jack were here now how happy I'd be.
The fighting back then was meant to be fun
A play fight that ended when Jack's life was gone.

So poor Jack is dead and alone I'm at last
Each day finds me cursing the life that had past.
Will I see Jack again? Will I hear him call?
Will he come back again by the cemetery wall?

Can you ever see a time?
Frank Condon.

Can you ever see a time when there are no priests at all?

Where ever can we shrive ourselves? Beside the "Wailing Wall."

Then what about forgiveness, where can we then get peace?

Where now with absolution, we can get that through our priest

So give your sons a talking to and ask for help divine.

So we can be prepared if there ever comes a time!

No one listened.
Frank Condon.

No one ever goes there now, not like in days of yore.

The hinges have all rusted up we can't get through the door.

The ivy all around it has grown so firm and stout,

As if to stop us going in though no one will I doubt.

Yet looking back I wonder, though it's not so long ago

I can still see smiling faces and hear the organ blow.

The scene that I am seeing is in a forward time

When people stop believing in your god and in mine.

When people all around the world don't heed him anymore

When the computer it is king and it will keep our score!

CEMETERY POEM
Frank Condon

Saint Stephen's Cemetery is not a lonely place, for there throughout the day
Folks they come to visit, and some, to kneel and pray.
And in it's midst a stone built church, the centre point of all
An imposing entrance leads one in, and its guardian is a wall.

Is the wall put there to keep souls in? I doubt if that is so,
For all the folk that's resting there, from labours long ago
And why then is a wall put there? To keep all noise at bay?
To give this place an air of quiet, while visitors kneel to pray?

This place to me is special, for resting 'neath each sod
Are dear friends and relations that, surely rest with God?
Near that little hallowed church is, where my parents lay

I should visit there more often, if only to kneel and pray

A granddad too and a young nephew, lay sleeping here below
How sad it was at his tender years, God called he had to go
A new comer to this place of rest, though sudden and severe
Is the husband of my sister, called at Eastertide of year?

How sad it is to see each name, on tombstones high and low
My friends are numbered many here, in plots and numbered row
How sad it is to see tall grass, on forgotten burial places
How sorry I am remembering, for I can't recall their faces

I stand alone in reverie, I an old man standing here
I try so hard to be cheerful, when down my face a tear
My eyes are brimming over, it's time for me say
I go but I'll return again, if only an Ave to pray.

Life's circle.
Frank Condon.

Well, God be with my childhood days, for days like those were good,

on summer days we walked or lazed, running deep into the dark wood.

In sunlit fields, on the old bog road, with shoeless feet we trod,

we climbed huge trees, high amongst the leaves much nearer here to God.

Bird nesting then was all the rage and we hunted high and low,

we knew all birds by their coloured eggs from wren to coal black crow.

Each berried bush, each fragrant flower, each leaf betrayed each tree,

for names were not a need for us but was a sight to see.

The smallest animals we knew, we knew the fleetest hare,

oh God be with those bygone days I wish that they were here.

As the summer sun climbed lower and those crazy summer days,

were marked by crunchy coloured leaves, under foot in all marked ways.

When days were getting shorter as does the blackbird's song,

the hoary frosts of winter would be here before too long

A silent word of snow and frost, rotted leaves among,

the earth, like life itself, full circle then, had turned and then is gone.

Counting my blessings.
Frank Condon.

On Monday night as I slept lord, I had a terrible dream,

I could no longer see lord, life was a darkened scene.

Gone the beauty of summer showers, the wind that blow long grasses

In an instant from my sight the loveliness of lasses.

But I awoke next morning to notice a sunlight sky

And knelt to thank the lord that I still had sight of eye.

On Tuesday night once more dear lord my mind was filled with fears.

I could not hear a blessed thing how useless now my ears!

I'd miss the rushing waters, the lark's song in the morn'

How could I rise to meet you lord I would not hear Gabriel's horn.

But I awoke next morning to hear folks all around

And here I prostrate fall lord to thank the lord of sound.

On Wednesday night once more I dreamt and my dream was such

I could not feel my body lord I had lost my sense of touch.

I could not feel the heat or cold it was like my hands were numb

I could not travel through life like this oh lord what had I done.

But the morning sunlight crossed my bed until it touched my finger

I felt a warm glow again as the sun stopped there to linger.

Thursday ended very well as I blew out my candle

Nothing threatened me so far well, nothing I couldn't handle.

But I worried then when I couldn't smell as I snuffed the candle head

Where was the smell I got each night as I climbed into bed?

But morning came as it does each day to waken life anew

I was glad that I could smell again and lord it was thanks to you.

Oh lord how could I live a life without the smell of flowers

As I walk the summer meadows to spend some happy hours.

Come Friday night I'm thankful for all the gifts I've got

I could see and hear and smell and touch and best of all

could talk.

So let us then be thankful to the creator of those things

And ask when life is over if he could add a pair of wings.

Do you get the Picture?
Frank Condon

Our Tutor's a fella, a kind decent man; he does his best to teach everyone.

He searches to find ways to get us to write

For odd bits and pieces searches long days and night.

Last week well you know, when there were ten of us there,

Round oddly shaped tables where each had a chair

Pictures were our subjects, a street in old Amsterdam

Showing lots of fine ladies, no sign of a man.

Well, maybe there was one that I could not see

'Twas dark, it was raining much too dark for me.

This crowded scene devoid of much light

'Twas daytime I'm sure, yes I'm sure I am right.

The scene looked busy a scene from long ago

ladies in long velveteen dresses and each sporting a boa.

They all seemed so happy all seemed so fine

With high feathered bonnets and bustles behind.

What caused them to gather what caused them to meet?

Was it that there was a theatre in this cobbled street?

Was it in those shops, selling beauty rare?

Charging low, low prices, was that why they were there?

Shop windows all had panes made of bubble glass

A Dickensian scene right out of the past.

Pity the weather it didn't match their mood

Far above their heads hung a black storm cloud.

A hackney carriage in the picture I see

No sign of a driver! Is he out looking for me?

I become part of the picture and I am there

I'm frightened and worried is there no one to care?

The lightning did flash and the thunder did roll

Frightened the Mare who is heavy with foal.

The Mare lifts her head her eyes wide with fright

A foam flecked mouth as she shot off in flight.

A swirl of skirts and then the sounds of rushing feet

A high-pitched scream now's a very different street.

The Mare dashes onward full stricken bound

Two kids and their mother is stuck to the ground.

The run-away Mare, to this horrified crowd

In one long shriek they shouted aloud.

A tall dark figure from nowhere is seen

He runs like the wind as he enters that scene.

Fleet of foot is this man as is the Mare

He grabs her halter and stops her there

The family is safe the crowd raise a shout

And to top it off the sun comes out.

I am their hero they'll have no other

I was that close to death that it makes me shudder.

All in the picture are pleased you see

I am their hero yes it is me.

From a simple picture this story has grown

To become a tale of old Amsterdam town.

Hans Christian Anderson I never did see

Do you think yourself that I am he?

Doolin
Frank Condon.

At a village in Clare, while on holiday there,
The sun was shining bright.
The days were grand, in that lovely land
Ceile music filled the night

The colleens too, were fair to view,
I wish I was young once more
I tell you that, for I love the craic
Standing by Mc Dermot's door.

It's a musical place, they're a very fine race,
Those folk that live by the sea.
There's no sign of care, in the County Clare
Well, none that I could see.

From far away, we came to stay,
'Twas serious stuff no foolin,
In our cottage small, with blue-stone wall,
We spent our days in Doolin.

There were people there, from God knows where,
 All coming for the craic.
The big the small, we met them all,

All taking their memories back.

But memories all, and stories tall,
Even some that was never told
I spoke about, the music and shout
But folks there too were old.

Each Doolin Street, was very sweet,
Nestling at the foot of a hill
It is a fright, to walk down each night,
Worse still, when you've had your fill.

Of the black and strong, for one could go wrong
Just climbing the road securing,
A safety pace, from that hilly place
From that village known as Doolin.

Now Doolin town, it is renown,
For music and for dancing
For drinking too, done by a few
But most they went for chancing.

Chancing there was, I know because,
I went looking for a wife
For I've heard it said, they are good with their head
And loving all of their life.

I looked around, but too young I'd found,
Too young to be a farmer
Given good advise, they told me twice,
I should go to Lisdunvarna.

I got in a state, looking for a mate,
In fact I was fairly droolin
When I went each night, sure it was a fright
Trying to find a wife in Doolin.

Now Doolin Town, it will astound,
And if you are young at heart
For young and old, for the brave and bold,
You can't tell them apart.

For in Doolin you know, you walk very slow
We're enchanted one and all
there all sang and danced, as though entranced
In the pubs both big and small.

Now Doolin town, it will astound

in fact it is entrancing
For there's music there, and a magic air
For jigging and for dancing.

If you like the craic, then you'll come back,
And you might think I'm foolin
To that tiny hub called Mc Diarmid's pub
and the village known as Doolin.

Friends
Frank Condon

It's a very wise man who can have a friend, who will neither borrow nor will he lend.

For there are some people without a doubt, who will loan an umbrella when the sun is out.

Only to ask for it back again, as soon as there is a sign of rain.

So if your friends are like none of those, then think you're self-lucky I suppose.

For friends who borrow when not in need, we tend not to see them as friends indeed.

But when you are given a helping hand, when things haven't turned out quite as planned,

Now those are the friends that are of worth, and should be regarded as the salt of the earth.

Go find your Dad
Frank Condon

One fine spring morning in County Clare,
I saw a man sat on a chair
By a fine old cottage built of stone
The man looked sad and all alone.

His big sad eyes looked out to sea
Toward the setting sun alone sat he.
The sight of a liner caused him to stir
Though far at sea and but a blur.

He left his seat in the setting sun
Glad at last that the ship had come.
For his love he waited in America
Now fifteen years since she went away.

She said she'd return once again
But for fifteen years he waited in vain.
But now his hopes were high once more
The liner was heading in for shore.

He could see this girl with raven hair
And stroked his eye to brush a tear.
The ship it docked he was waiting there

To be greeted and kissed by this maiden fair.

"I am your daughter", she did softly say,
Mother was pregnant when she went away.
She died of a fever and when nearly mad,
When she told me softly, "Go find your Dad."

Good-bye Digger.
Frank Condon.

From far across the seas they came to dig for alluvial Gold.

To this hell-hole-land where sweat and tears combine to make men old.

To this land where sweat and thirst held sway in that far off lonesome place,

Where tired old men with broken backs no longer show their pace.

Where children born 'neath those sunlit skies to women bent at work,

Were buried just born, as were their mums, where disease and famine lurk.

Where children young as five and six were sent to work each day,

'The Picky boys' of the conveyor belts for them there was little pay.

From far off Cornwall they came where lead and tin no more is found,

To that land of warm sunshine where entire lifetimes were spent under ground.

With hopeful hearts of a better life they traversed that briny plain

Some died, some lived and some were born but none of all remain?

The Gold's no more the copper too lie in that watery grave,

The pumps were stopped the water rose no money could be made.

The price of copper fell away and as the prices dwindled

The pumps were disassembled and orders were rescinded

The gold's still there the copper too but far, far under ground,

The diggers have all wandered where other work they found.

Where now the men whose backs were bent beneath that burning sun

When money was earned in honest toil with no thought of riches or fun.

Where now those slavish women who born-ed and worked and died?

Beside those men with broken backs whom they cherished with loving pride?

In high-rise office blocks they work no longer under ground

Oh how their lives have changed since that alluvial gold was found.

Hard Times in London
Frank Condon

'Tis hard ould times in London to my regret I've found
sleeping rough, sometimes 'twas tough, in doorways all around.
With a paper box for shelter and an empty bottle by my side
Through the shame of my undoing finding nowhere now to hide.

In loneliness I wander to my kipper under a railway arch
Where folk like me, full desolate seek, fluid to ease our parch.
In my early days when I was young, I always had the sub'
For the crack was good in Cricklewood and I always had some food.

But money filtered through my hands, no savings then I'm thinking

Folks didn't say much in Shepherds Bush, all far too busy drinking?
The years flew by trying to survive, hard work was killing me,
My poor back ached, for moneys sake but still I could not see?

And still the drink continued boys how the publicans can pull them,
It was no joke when stony broke finding 'nare a friend in Fulham.
In Hammersmith in the Wroughton House I thought I reached my end,
When a policeman he, directed me, me thinking I'd found a friend.

But when morning came I still feel the shame, I scratched from toe to head

'Twasn't very nice I was covered in lice, that's something that I dread?

Now tell me friend, where will this all end? Will I be alive tomorrow?

I wish I were home and stop been alone, I'm filling my life with sorrow.

Hayfever
Frank Condon

I wake each morn, all forlorn
And I sneeze near twenty snorts
Each flower head, whether yellow or red
Scatter pollen 'till my nose hurts.
Now grasses tall, with seeds do fall
Under cutting blades so easy
While billowing dust, up my nose is snuffed
Make me convulse like crazy.

Air pollution unclean, rises up unseen
But this unseen dust is clever
To achieve its aim, they gave it a name
Which troubles us all 'Hayfever'.

While clear blue sky, with tears fill my eye
And makes my nose all runny
In the house I stay, never out to play
While everyone thinks its funny?
Where streamlets run, Beavers do have fun
How I wish I were a Beaver?
Whether meadow or lake, tablets I must take
To ease this curse 'Hayfever'.

I cry my way through each summer's day,

With runny nose so swollen
My vision is marred, I see nothing but stars
Oh God, how the mighty have fallen.
What do scientists do, I ask of you?
Will they ever find a lever?
To ease this case, where the human race
Can be cured of this 'Hayfever?-

The High Hill.
Air: Spansil Hill
Frank Condon.

I awoke last night at midnight; I was sad and all alone.

For I dreamt I was back home again in old New Ross my home,

I crossed the Barrow River on the old bridge I remember it still

And I headed up through Bridge Street on my way to the High Hill.

I stopped beside the Royal hotel to catch some memories

Where looking down through North Street the Tolstel I could see.

I waited there without care, as if I had time to kill

For I loved that ould spot, and why would I not, at foot of the High Hill.

I passed by Hanrahan's public house I worked there as a lad
Looking after Jimmy's greyhounds were it four or five that he had?
The 'Mile bush Flyer' was one of them and I feared it would come to harm
When he broke away one stormy day the thunder it caused him alarm.

Tearing down the Goat hill it gave me a chill, empty collar still in my hand.
'Twas by the pink rock, they found Jimmy's dog, and him sitting on the sand!
I was sacked from there, as I'd had my share before Jimmy had a chance to kill
How the boys all laughed and girls all clapped at the bottom of the High Hill.

Then on past Maher's bake house where a baker I thought I'd be

From early morn 'till dewey eve I worked almost for free
But Maher changed his mind after he did find, eating cakes 'till I'd had me fill
Up in Barrack lane where he did complain, but for that I'd be working there still.

The cakes were for sale Mr. Maher did wail and so I got the sack
I greatly did plead for my family's need but he wouldn't have me back.
So I joined the unemployable lads and I'm sure I'd be there still
By the Royal Hotel, stories we would tell, at the foot of the High hill!

Through South Street then I did proceed, meeting folks I knew now and then.
And I stopped awhile, for it made me smile, beside the L.N.

As a messenger boy I was full of joy, they supplied me with a bike
I loved that job, they only paid a few bob, but that was a job I did like.

Until one day when me brakes gave way, down Cross lane I was going fast
Going faster still, at the foot of that hill and through O'Brian's showroom glass.
L.N. paid for the glass, after that big smash, then told me to take a hike
I was fired from that place, with a bleeding cut face, and they took away their bike.

In Priory Place, sure it's a disgrace, they closed the old Tanyard down
I remember well, aye and folks will tell, how they missed that hooter's sound

I recrossed by the quay, on my very short stay, of walking I've had my fill
All the friends I would need, my sore feet did lead, to the bottom of the High Hill.

At daybreak I awoke me poor heart nearly broke for those memories were still in me head
Not a sight nor a sound of old New Ross town as me wife pushed me out of the bed
But I'll still travel back if only for the craic when New Ross is eight hundred years old
From this very cold place, I can no longer face for Alaska is far too cold.

The first day at school.
Frank Condon.

"Be a brave and honest soldier," the mother told her lad as she brushed the fringe out of his eyes, which to day looked very sad.

The soldier nodded bravely as he buttoned up his Mac' he placed his satchel on his shoulder and never once looked back.

He would face the war zone bravely; he would not look a fool but like all mothers she was anxious on her son's first day at school.

She hurried him along the road it wouldn't do if they were late and the mother's heart was breaking as he passed through the gate.

To day she should be happy as she watched him march away for five long years she'd waited, for the coming of this day. She'd tutored him and scolded him and watched her young son grow all in preparation for the day when he would go.

She worried had she failed him, in some, in any way preparing him to stand alone, in the world and have his say. She had tried to make him bolder, to be secure amongst the flock and in times of adversity, to be steady as a rock.

Her world was full of worries, would he learn the golden rule? It was a day so full of worries, on her son's first day at school.

Hopefully.
Frank Condon

I rose this morning early, the sun was shining bright
I had lived to see the dawning, got through another night.
I dressed and had some breakfast, my heart was feeling gay
I went outside and walked a while, sort of savouring the day.

A day so full of sunshine, where everything seemed so bright
So different from the darkness that envelope us each night
For each days like a beginning , anew start every morn
Forget what's happened the day before for each daylight lessens the harm

The sick the sore the weary, they dread each long dark night
]Alone with dark and suffering so filled with dread and fright
But come the morning sunshine to vanish terror and fear
That friendly knock upon the door just to say a friend is here.

How do I see you
Frank Condon

You are environmental and all around see
You turn up to comfort like a warm blanket is to me
A building too is likened you or maybe just a book
A season warm and cosy, a rocking chair in a nook

As a vehicle I see you, a motorbike of course
With sound that's oh so throaty or a cowboy on a horse.
A sunset red and rosy a morning fair and quite
The soft yellow of moonlight a quite silence like the night

You are the warm hand of friendship a love to satisfy
A love to last a lifetime and I not know the reason why!

I once had a girlfriend
Frank Condon

Parady

I once had a girlfriend from the top Irish town
The one fault she had, always putting me down.

Chorus

<u>***AH but still I love her I can't forget her***</u>

<u>And I'll go with her tomorrow bye and bye.</u>

She kicks in our front door and orders me out
By the smell of her breath she'd been drinking stout.

Chorus
We go up to Kavanagh's for a happy night out
I order some whiskey but she wanted stout!

Chorus

Her right hook just tapped me, I fell to the floor
grabbing hold of my heels, she threw me out the door.

Chorus

I cooked her some pigs feet, once her delight
But this started a big row, that went on all night.

Chorus

I bought her a new coat the dearest of all
But she swore that I'd bought it off 'ould cheap John' stall?

Chorus

Now bottles of Guinness are stashed everywhere
And once they are empty, she doesn't have a care.

**Ah but now I don't love her, for I love her brother
And I will go with him where ever he goes.**

I remember I remember
FRANK CONDON

I remember I remember, the house where I was born,

As the wind blew down the chimney it woke me every morn'

The tin roof rattled when it rained which made us cover our heads,

for we were only babies then that lay listening in our beds.

The windows rattled also as round our house it blew,

it whistled underneath our door and through a crack or two.

The walls were built of mud and stone, and the rain it did soak through,

no need for chalk to draw on walls, a piece of stick would do.

Our kitchen floor it was the earth, the same as was outdoors,
the bedrooms too they were all the same, and so were all our floors.
We did not have two up two down, we had two rooms that's all
We never had a bathroom, central heating or a hall.

We did we had a front door, which was always open wide
If only to let the smoke out that always was inside.
You see it was our chimney, it really was a joke
When the wind came from one direction
it smothered the house with smoke.

I must say about our fireplace from where the smoke began,

to keep the fire a going, air was supplied with a hand cranked fan.

This caused our fire to flourish and warm us through the night,

to make the tea and boil the spuds, it even gave us light.

The fire provided comfort, as round our blazing hearth,

The Rosary would be said each night and of course we all took part.

We all lived there together, as happy as can be,

Three brothers and a sister my mum and dad and me.

My father had a gramophone, a present from his wife

He played it every Sunday, the best thing in his life

He would turn a handle to wind it up, then it went round and round.

A horn was there a big one, so we could hear the sound.

'Till something took his fancy, he wanted it I guess,
A marvellous invention, it was called a wireless.
We listened to it each Sunday as the door was on the latch
The neighbours came from mile around to listen to the football match.
But now we're in a semi with a bathroom and a hall,
do we miss those awful times now? Not at all at all.

If I was Blind?
Poem.
Frank Condon.

If I was Blind and could not see, what do you think would happen to me?

If I was deaf and could not hear, it wouldn't stop me from drinking beer!

If I was limbless and couldn't walk, I'd sit all day and talk and Talk.

If I were fat and heavy on my feet, hundreds of thin folk I would meet.

If I was young and in my prime, I'd pity the old folk all the time!

If I were old and not too strong, Would I pity the children 'cause they were young?

But worst of all if I were blind the world around me I'd never find.

If

Unless some person with a seeing eye, described to me the earth and sky.
The colour that was buttercup, the danger of an unseen drop?
The colour of the wind and rain, the walking down a country lane!
The smiling face of a happy child, yes been blind can drive one wild.

If I were wealthy and not poor, the world could gather at my door.
I'd feed the hungry all day long and send them away with a happy song.
If I was dumb I'd ask the lord but how could I ask without saying a word?
Still I'd whistle a tune so happy and gay to brightness the sadness of my day.

was blind and couldn't hear I'd wear a smile from ear to ear.

I'd listen in my silent place, still with a smile upon my face.

With eyelids closed there I could hide, from a world of terror deep inside.

All fears and sorrows all there on file, Yes been blind can make one wild!!!

In a hospital ward!
Frank Condon

The night was dark the light was dim
Should have left the house but I stayed in.

The reasons why I must confess

I have no knowledge but I can guess.

You see I think I'm afraid at night

As a child in hospital I'd a terrible fright.

In a hospital ward I was all-alone,

Missing my family so far from home.

The night was windy, such a gale,

A tree blew down I felt very frail.

Would the windows hold out that windy dark?

That was threatening me with rain so stark?

A ghost passed by all shimmering bright

Outside my window on that terrible night.

I called aloud and the ghost returned,

Glowing so brightly how my eyes burned.

Then another ghost came into sight,

It too from head to toe in white?

My poor little heart was beating fast,

If there were others, then the lightning flashed,

The softest voice spoke my name, not course

A light came on, it was a kindly nurse?

It couldn't be done, they said.
Frank Condon.

I tackled this thing that couldn't be done,

The training scheme though rough it was fun,

The cold and heat, the sweat and pain,

Early mornings, no sleep was a strain.

The aloneness of the long days walk

No time to ponder or stop and talk.

The sun came up and set each day,

I was still trying there was no other way,

The road grew longer now all up hill,

I set my face and went wit a will,

My story is true believe me son,

For I tackled this thing that couldn't be done.

I rose each morning at break of day,

Glad was I to be on my way,

I strove to do better than the day before,

Was there another like me from shore to shore?

My pride forbade me I'd not complain,

To take those pills to ease my pain,

Other do I know, I've heard it said

But I put such thoughts right out of my head.

I've tried, I'd failed by that last setting sun,

When I tackled this thing that couldn't be done.

Just killing time.
Frank Condon.

At 69 I'm wondering, indeed I have no fear.

When 70 come a calling I hope I'll still be here?

When I was just a lad of 10 I thought that I was old,

Just then poor men of 70 were lying dead and cold.

Workers then were sixteen and drew a weekly wage,

Working hard for 50 hours they'll never see old age.

Men of 30 bent and grey with a family still to feed

A wife, a house and several kids 'twas tough they all agreed.

At 40 life was still the same and sometimes maybe worse,

'Twas not an uncommon sight then to be riding in a hearse.

I don't mean in the driving seat but in a box of pine,

They didn't think 'twould end like this when they were 39.

Chances then grew slimmer as each working day it passed,

Staring Black Death in the face you knew you'd never last.

But somehow maybe somewhere, the sun was shinning bright,

'Twasn't the days that frightened me, but the coldness of black night.

The fifties came and went so quick I didn't notice time,

'Till one fine day I woke up, at the age of sixty nine!

Song air; mountain Dew.
Frank Condon.

Chorus

Oh-----The craic is good in Kavanagh's pub
for so I've heard it say,
Where they sing 'till dawn without a yawn
Going home at the break of day.

On the brow of the hill, men have their fill
Of porter, stout and ale
There the company's grand I understand
And the women are hearty and hale.
Chorus

On Saturday night, there the lights burn bright
As music fills the air.
John Condon sings and there's other things
And I'm sure it's a grand affair.
Chorus

The beer is cheap, it will not keep
Not for another day!

So, they order more, its already in store,
Sure no one here drinks tay.
Chorus

This place it heaves, from floor to eaves
And not just on a Saturday night!
Pop up and see, if you don't believe me,
Then you'll know that I'm right?
               Chorus.

Oh--- the craic is good in Kavanagh's pub
for so I've heard them say'
Where the sing 'till dawn, never saw one yawn
Going home at the break of day.

Kitty The Hare
Frank Condon

When the wind blows cold in Ireland and your seated by the fire, there is nothing better they like there, there is nothing more admired.

Than the travelling woman's stories to take and heal their care, and best of all to tell them is the one called Kitty the Hare.

From childhood days I heard them, I listened without fear or fright, her stories always started, "I've a strange story to tell to night."

She would tell of stories from far away that she heard while at the fair, and the stories that she heard there was retold by Kitty the Hare.

Now some were funny and some were sad you listened for she could tell, the stories that you listened to you knew of the people very well.

For around each fireside glowing as they around her chair "God bless the hearers this very night," were the words of Kitty the Hare.

The tea was made and the currant bread was handed all around and through it all nothing was heard except the speakers sound.

For in the morning she'd be gone, gone in the fresh dawn air, the tail of her coat that was all you'd see, aye, that was Kitty the Hare.

At the halfway house they'd gather when they heard she was on her way, when men and women and children would come to hear her say.

"The strangest story I'll tell you and you might think it quare," oh boys could she tell a story, that one called Kitty the Hare.

The world I've travelled over far from my native shore the stories that I've heard around they number by the score But of all the foreign stories there is nothing to compare, with, "God bless the hearers this very night," when spoke by Kitty the Hare.

Landscapes, Yeah Maybe.
Frank Condon.

I have walked on the gold coast but no gold was there,

From Table Rock Mountain the view it was fair

I climbed Lion Head Mountain and what did I see?

Only Cape Town below, on the flat by the sea!

On Sugarloaf Mountain, a breathless young man

Sat cooling him self with a flat stone for a fan

What had he gone for? The view, so said he

But nothing was there worth viewing for me!

I next went to Cape Cod, a wonderful place

To harvest cranberries for people with taste.

But while I was down there the leaves turned to gold

The summer had ended and the wind turned cold.

As New York was near by to the heights I did climb

'twas on Empire State building that I made up my mind.

That in all of my travels I never did see

A landscape as nice as my home by the sea.

Why had I left there I questioned my heart?

To see the great landscapes as painted in art!

I had seen lovely landscapes but still in my mind

I know that the best ones I had left them behind.

But landscapes are plenty in every place

But beauty I see in my Grandchildren face

As they gather around me the short and the tall

I would rather admire them than landscapes in all!

Life's circle.
Frank Condon.

Well, God be with my childhood days, for days like those were good, on summer days we walked or lazed, running deep into the dark wood.

In sunlit fields, on the old bog road, with shoeless feet we trod, we climbed huge trees, high amongst the leaves much nearer here to God.

Bird nesting then was all the rage and we hunted high and low, we knew all birds by their coloured eggs from wren to coal black crow.

Each berried bush, each fragrant flower, each leaf betrayed each tree, for names were not a need for us but was a sight to see.

The smallest animals we knew, we knew the fleetest hare, oh God be with those bygone days I still wish that they were here.

As the summer sun climbed lower and those crazy summer days, were marked by crunchy coloured leaves, under foot in all marked ways.

The days are getting shorter now, as does the blackbird's song, the hoary frosts of winter would be here before ere long

A silent word of snow and frost, of rain and rotted leaves among, the earth, like life itself, full circle then, had turned and then is gone.

Love's unkind.
Frank Condon

We planned to elope when nigh time came,

We loved, 'twas enough, where was the shame?

Long sloping hillside under a glowering sky,

Cold bitter rain fell as we pass by.

With love we walked the endless track,

Just going forward no looking back.

The ladder just reached her windowsill,

In flowery dress she waited so still.

I whisked her on to my swiftest steed,

While holding the horse, her sister Breed.

A shot rang out, her father's gun?

He shot the horse, the deed was done.

We ran and ran 'till our legs gave out

We hid in a drain, heard her father shout!

We daren't look up 'cause weren't bold

The time passed slowly,'Twas bitter cold.

As we hugged each other and died that night

In a drain by the road where we first caught sight.

Middlewood
Frank Condon

The show would go to "Middlewood."
The show would go to "Middlewood" of that

there was no doubt,

If only to find the snags and faults and then

to iron them out.

We didn't expect no problems, up to then

we'd missed no line,

our confidence was very high and everything

would be fine.

So at our club while waiting, we'd rehearse our play once more,

until the sound of transport was heard outside the door.

We rehearsed our way to "Middlewood" there really was no fuss,

we sat amongst our props and things, while "Matty" drove the bus.

When we got to the theatre, Matty had us there within a tick,

We unloaded all our luggage and got costumed very quick.

The stage was set already that did save us some time.

Positions please, and curtain, still everything was fine.

The lines they started going wrong! The director paced about!

Then came the crucial moment, and the lights they never went out!

Now where the hell is Martin? We cannot find the door!

They will surely throw us out now, and let us back no more.

The curtain dropped to save us all, to end our one act play,

But our "problems" if you could call them that, just did not go away.

The variety acts were chaos, the costumes were all wrong!

With "flea act" and "mind readers" on stage in the middle of a song!

Now, some were dressed to do their act, to do their very best,

To give a good impression and be better than the rest.

"Its time for bed," then someone said, "We'll end the show right here."

Oh, I'm not ready for finale, oh dear, oh dear, oh dear.

The panic in both dressing rooms, I'd end it if I could,

But I'll never forget the night we took our show to "Middlewood."

MISERY.
Frank Condon.

The day was sad the day was wet
How much worse can a bad day get?
Then from the rooftops a frightening shout
'This country's plagued with foot and mouth.

Swine fever is ended, under control
That worried us it shocked our soul
When chicken pest was all the rage
It seemed to last a very long age.

Salmonella too attacked our gut
When we complained we got no soot
But still our people are very put out
While this county's plagued with foot and mouth.

Then came to the fore the MMR scare
This worried poor mommas everywhere
The three in one needle became a schism
Rumours proclaimed it caused autism.

Science took one pace forward then two back
They're not even sure they're on the right track
Do they really know what it's all about
Why this county is plagued with foot and mouth?

CJD too they can't find a name
All still pondering looking for blame
So we've killed all the cattle sheep and eggs
They haven't yet started on us with two legs

There is still the bread and of course the beans
But there's modified crops that are not yet seen
The humble spud we'll keep quiet about
While this country still uneasy about foot and mouth.

Musket on the wall
Frank Condon

The inside of our cabin was cosy warm and snug
Our floorboards they were bare we didn't have a rug
The walls were solid timber hewn and shaped by father's hand
The chimney tall was built of stone all gathered from our land.

A musket hangs above the fire a musket made to last
'Twas used in far off troubled times but those times now have passed
No rust it showed, a well oiled piece a treasure to behold
Oh how I wish that it could speak what stories would unfold.

Beside that musket, in pride of place a headdress of Indian hue

A trophy no, a prize maybe or was it something new?
A bloodstain on the cabin floor I'd not seen that before
I should remember but I can't inside the cabin door.

The door was stout and thick and hard 'twas made from old pitch pine
It kept us safe, shut out the dark and stood the test of time
But something bad had entered in destroying our peaceful life
Leaving me without a mother and Paw without a wife.

We buried Maw on the hillside and secured again the busted door
Then settled down to lead a life without a mother on our floor
So Time it passed and each long day I would hear dad's musket roar
As evening came and Paw came home we had meat and game galore.

But game got scarce and animals all seemed to disappear
The mountainside too peaceful now no game, no food, no deer
I left that cabin to wander sad to leave my mountain home
And sad to meet the world outside while leaving Paw alone.

That musket still hangs above the fire when I return to find
That the Paw I'd loved in childhood the Paw I'd left behind
Was nowhere to be seen no more but a busted splintered door?
Was that my old Paw's blood I saw that stain upon the floor?

New Line to town
Frank Condon

The water butt at the side of our house
It froze in winter to solid cold ice.
The barrel originally was filled with tar
When we built our road but we had no car.

I remember well as we trod to school
The road did smell it made us drool.
New stone quite sharp cut childish feet
A road so long you'd never meet.

A neighbour farmer when going to town
Would shatter the early morning sound.
All noise created by crunching stone
Filled him with feelings he was not alone

But he wished him self to be on his way home
For he still had fields that needed sown
And trees and bushes to trim alone
And cattle's milk to take to town.

The numerous fields still left to till
By father he liked a nice straight drill
But a difficult task while working up hill
If he didn't have help he be there still.

All that was many a year ago
When life was sweet and things were slow.
Not like to day 'tis a noisy place
With tractor and cars all over the place.

It started so easy for I have found
The thing we done? Build a road to town
For now folks come from all around
To drive up our road they like the sound

Of crunching stone and the smell of tar
With windows open to breath the air
 not knowing our road doesn't go anywhere!!

Nothing Lasts.
Frank Condon.

I WALKED ALONG A ROAD TO DAY,
WHERE NO ONE SAW ME NO WORD I SAY.
A ROAD I'D TRAVELLED IN THE LONG GONE BY
WHAT BROUGH ME HERE I HEAVE A SIGH.

To walk my childhood days again
Just to remember to put to pen?
Those wondrous years with family all
To gaze once more on our family hall.

What was there standing left to see?
No house but a fondly remembered chestnut tree.
That chestnut standing oh so bare
A silent sentinel still standing there.

The house of birth built strong with stone

All now is gone I stand alone.
The laughter times are silent gone
Why stand I here I must move on.

And yet I linger hoping to grasp
Just one single memory from my past.
But all is bare, all is cold
Could it be too that I am old?
Why stand I here like a thing from the past
It is but shameful how nothing lasts.

Now.
Frank Condon.

Now is a most peculiar time, there is nothing happening to put in Rhyme.

Now, if I was writing of long ago, my pen would fly, I'd have something to show.

Now is neither future or past, it's a time peculiar, it doesn't last.

Now is here and then it's gone, yet **now** is with us all day long?

Now where did I put that thought I had, I could do with it **now** I need it bad?

Now where is my youth? In the long ago?

Now is old age, it is very slow.

Now is the time when I climb the stair, but what am I doing when I get up there?

Now is the time I need to know? Do I stay or do I go?

Now it's too late for without haste, I have wet my self I'm a total disgrace.

Now my Zimmer frame is far too fast, if it keeps this up I'll never last!

Now the time has come for me I fear, I've lived my life I'm outa here.

O.N.E.T poem.
Frank Condon

O.N.E.T itself seek, neither fortune nor fame

Just a gathering of ex-soldiers, who from Ireland came.

They served their country, both home and away

Sailors, airmen and soldiers, and of course the F.C.A

We now have a banner, to march under once more

we old soldiers and sailors, that once marched to the fore

The airmen among us, we see no reason why

They too can't join us, when down from the sky.

To meet have the craic, share memories some old

When we all served the colours green white and gold

To talk of old times, have the odd day out

Sit down to a meal, with a full glass of stout.

To invite all our wives, to meet one and other

Under the O.N.E.T banner, like a band of brother.

O.N.E.T is the place, for every Tom Dick and Da

Oglaigh Naisiunta Na Heireann teoranta.

ONET

O.N.E.T itself seeks neither fortune nor fame
Just an assemblage of ex-soldiers who from Ireland came.
That served their country both home and away
Sailors, airmen and soldiers and of course the FCA.

We now have a banner to march under once more
Us old sailors and soldiers that marched to the fore.
The men flying above us we see no reason why
They too can't join us when then come down from the sky.

To meet have the craic, share memories of old
When we all served the colours of green white and gold.
To talk of old times and share the odd days out
To sit down to a good meal and a bottle of stout.

To invite all the wives to meet one another
Under the O.N.E.T banner like a band of brothers.
O.N.E.T is the place for every Tom Dick and Da

Oglaigh Naisiunta Na heeireann teoranta.

Ode to Tommy, my friend.
Frank Condon

A good friend indeed, when we were in need,

Whenever we hit London town

He was a true friend, yes that was his intend,

And nice chap to have around.

His home, though not new, was a pleasure to view

Talking of times that are past,

Discussing old days an old man's craze,

How the days of our youth went so fast.

But then there was strife, when Tommy lost his wife

And sadness did prevail.

We still kept in touch, though it wasn't very much,

Still, I need to tell the tale.

When we set off that day, 'twas a long, long way

To lay his good wife at rest.

When a terrible pain, added to our strain,

Doubled over my, wife well, you've guessed.

Now our journey did stop, off the bus we did hop,

To take my poor wife back home.

This whole case was bad, leaving us very sad,

And leaving poor Tommy alone.

Time has since past, 'twas March time at last,

with everything sorted and well,

When on Patrick's day, we with Tommy did stay,

This is still the same story I tell.

When the sun it shone bright, it was a delight

A wonderful memorable day,

We walked the long walk, and to friends we did talk,

White Orange and Green all the way.

On Saint Patrick's parade, with very little shade, heading

down the South Bank to the Wheel.

We smiled to be there, green and gold everywhere,

We felt great, and how would you feel?

The parade snaked along, the crowd, what a throng?

We Irish, we owned London Town.

Now that was some sight, 'twas surely a fright

With Tommy and I just fooling around.

We arrived at the Wheel, no discomfort did feel,

Together we'd marched side by side

Then on the way back still full of the craic,

Were two old men who would never have cried.

From New Ross we came, that's all we can claim,

To remain forever as friends

We went through the bad times and also the sad times,

Content with whatever God sends.

Still very good friends, whatever life sends

We will ague but never get vext.

Through life we must plod, far from the old sod

Taking whatever comes next.

Ode To Father Burke
Frank Condon

So now father Burke you are leaving

and we know that you're happy at least

But where ever you go we would like you to know

That you make a fine Parish Priest.

We have rested secure in the knowledge

That from Satan were safe from that beast

For we were kept on the straight and the narrow

By Father Burke who was our Parish Priest.

But now in the dark we will flounder

For his guidance to us have decreased

Though your gone father Burke we'll remember

You were one of the best as our Priest.

So rally the parish of St Marys

Send him of with a wish and a feast

We were happy to meet him,

shake his hand and to greet him

So goodbye now to our Parish Priest.

Old age.
Frank Condon.

As the time of our pension approaches and we near the best time of our life,

As we step through our sixties still partners, we're still together my self and my wife.

On the day we gave ourselves to each other, sure it's now in the grey mists of time.

Through the good and the bad times together, I tell you we're still doing fine.

There were times though we very near parted, my entire fault of course she did say, if I'd listened to her and took notice and we would not be together to day.

Some day we will live in the country, a beautiful cottage I see with roses a climbing all over just the place for my 'Missus' and me.

I can picture a sweet little cottage at the end of a small country lane we will live there together and happy, secure from the frost and the rain.

Our Kind of love.
Frank Condon

I find no wrong in loving you
Your love can do no harm
I do not mean to trouble you
But offer my strong right arm.

To hold you oh so firmly
And protect you through the night
To offer love and guidance
And hopefully do what's right.

There is no crime in loving you
A loving light like yours
I could spend eternity in wondering
The years, the months, the hours.

I need a love like yours dear
With which to travel on
Your smile your kind caresses
Are warmer than the sun.

Through dark of night I'll hold you tight
And stay there safe 'till dawn.
Each light of day to rise and say
I'll love you from now on.

In the pauper's ground?
Frank Condon.

I lie alone beneath this sod,
Will no one pray for me to God?
In this cold ground where I lie
No tears be shed not even a sigh.
My bones are cold I'm full of fear
How did I come to end up here?

When I was young the girls did say,
To each entreaty, 'I should go far away.'
For a wife I searched I looked afar,
From Wexford Town to Mullingar.
My bones are cold I'm full of fear
How did I come to end up here?

I found a damsel who gave me love.
Our marriage was blest from up above.
But her heart was fickle as was her mind
And so too it was maybe I was blind.
My bone are cold I'm full of fear
How did I come to end up here?

I challenged this man who took my wife
We met in a grove there was no light
He thrust I parried watched by my wife

With a murderous charge I took **her life.**
My bones are cold I'm full of fear.
How did I come to end up here?

They hung me high on the hanging tree
And there they left me for all to see.
The gawped and stared then took me down
And buried me deep in the Paupers ground.
My bones are cold I'm full of fear
Now you all know why I'm lying here.

"Philomath."
Frank Condon.

An interesting word is Philomath, a lover of learning it means,

An important word as it applies to most of us human beings.

Many other words we also learn and learn them off pat,

But never forget how it started it's because you're a Philomath.

Never mind the words of Shakespeare yes he was a clever chap,

He wrote and wrote in words sublime with a dictionary on his lap.

He wrote in a language difficult, difficult at least for me,

But because I am a Philomath I was willing to try to be,

Not another Shakespeare, for I could not afford the time

I'll just write my funny poetry and try to make it rhyme.

But don't forget I'm a Philomath a lover of learning they say,

So whatever it is I learning I'm learning it each and every day.

Picture a story.
Frank Condon.

"Who is this uncle Barney?" a small voice called out from the carpeted floor of the lounge.

"What is it Tim?" I asked.

"The person in this old black and white photo. It looks like a lady in posh clothes." I placed the hot coffee I had been drinking down on the coffee table near by, slid from my comfortable armchair on to the carpet beside my ten year-old nephew to get a closer look at the picture in his hand. The face looking back at me from the picture was both a delight and shock to me. I looked at my nephew and exclaimed with some surprise.

"Why it's the Princess," I told him.

My only nephew Timothy and his eleven year-old sister Louise, had been placed in my care by their mother before she hurried away to do her weekly shopping. Although my back garden was extensive with plenty of room to play the torrential rain had confined all of us indoors. For several minutes after they had arrived the T V had kept them amused but soon they became restless as all ten and eleven year-olds do. I had tried several games and an assortment of ways to occupy their wanderlust minds but to no avail. As was the case several times before the one thing that had never ceased to hold their interest was my collection of photographs. Photographs I had taken in my extensive trips around the world.

Each picture had a story behind it and of course it was up to me to unlock and tell that story. Most if not all of the pictures were of none or little consequence but it was up to me tell the story, true or false, made up or real that lay behind that photo.' My job was to colour and enhance and make the stories believable as well. The fact that I had never married and the fact that I had spent most of my life at sea, had placed me in some sort of adventurous world, a world I had created around my photographs on wet days such as to day.

Well, the story behind the old black and white photo' was no different from the other stories that had gone before. "A princess in waiting," I named her? The truth of course was that the girl in the photograph had at one time been a very dear friend of mine. A friend who promised to wait for me for one more year to wed, as I set off once more to sail round the horn of Africa to bring back the teas and silks from India and China. As we said our fond goodbye on the docks where we were both left low in spirit and eyes awash with wet salty tears. I never did see Amelia again and my life without her has always been a wasteland, where nothing but saltbush would grow. A vast expanse of plain where only an odd memory would surface now and again like an outcrop of rock protruding above that desolate wasteland. No one would ever succeed in lighting the flame of love in my life again after Amelia.

Now an old man, I entertained my nephew and niece with my hair-raising tales of wonders and adventures. Watching their faces and their eyes open wide with wonder whenever I was in mortal danger and clap their hands in glee at my narrow escapes only to end up in more danger several second later.

The storms at sea I had to endure in those far off south china seas. The huge sea serpents that inhabit those deep dark underwater caves, only surfacing whenever a ship was tossed and turned by the raging seas and the wild elements above in search of a meal. The shipwrecks I had in plenty to endure when I was never lucky enough to be cast ashore on some beautiful tropical island but cast up on to an island that was inhabited by never before heard of creatures that walked with the heads in the clouds. Or washed up on an island where I was constantly chased from place to place by fierce head hunters with long poles from which hung tiny human skulls that made uncanny sounds as they chased me.

The long days I had spent on long, lonely, stone strewn seashores, miles from civilisation having to live off wild honey and tame locusts. The cold dark nights too when a tropical storm soaked me through and the huge crashing waves that tried to drag me back into the water from which I had just crawled out of and on to dry land, a weary, shipwrecked sailor, far from home and friends. Then I opened my story with the words,

"And all this time the Tibetan Princess waited and waited for me to return. That poor girl had fallen in love with me when one day I arrived at her village, lost and almost out of my head. I had only just happened by chance to come across this small village high in the Andes Mountains. A poor lost soul of a sailor trying to find his way home. The royal family had taken me in, watered and fed me, according to their customs and beliefs.

It was only after I had spent a very comfortable night wrapped up in my soft Yak wool blankets that I discovered the Princess had not had any sleep at all that night? The king of Tibet, the Princess's father was not a well man and he had endured a painful night with no sleep with the Princess by his side at all times. I was later that day to learn that the poor king was afflicted with a Tibetan disease know as "Lumpsome back." The condition is said to be very upsetting for a king, as the condition was daily getting worse.

"Is there no cure to help the king?" I asked the Princess.

"The wise men of the council have heard of a cure," she told me, "but the ingredients to formulate the cure is far away in another country."

How far?" I asked.

"Far over those high mountains that surround Tibet," she sighed.

"May I enquire what those ingredients are?" I asked her Royal serene Highness. She looked at me with sad eyes before she made answer.

"I am told that they are wild honey and the most treasured item is a dried, tame locust." I had used those same items many times little knowing that they could have been a cure for "Lumpsome back."

"Sad as I am to say, your highness but I have only in the last few days in my travels eaten of those same items. Much grieved am I but because of my mental state I cannot recall where and when I partook of them. The Princess was saddened by my statement even more so than I was.

"I have more sad news to impart your highness," I told her "but now that I have fully recovered I should be wending my way homewards but I cannot leave you and your father without retracing my wandering steps hopefully to find the source of the wild honey and the tame locust." The Princess started to cry, where upon I reached into the pocket of my seaman's jacket to get my handkerchief. With a flourish I whipped out my handkerchief and bowing I presented it to the Lady.

In the process of been a gallant with my hanky something fell to the ground as I withdrew the hanky from my pocket. I bent down to retrieve that which had fallen from my pocket and to my delight I discovered that there was two items. One was non other than a dried tame locust and the other item was a small piece of honeycomb, which still contained a small amount of wild honey. Without delay the mixture was formulated and given to the ailing king who immediately had relief from the dreaded "Lumpsome back" disease.

Next morning the king, to show his gratitude wanted to marry his daughter and I thereby becoming king of Tibet in the process. I hummed and hawed and eventually told the king that I would first have to go home and get my parents permission before I could marry. While I was getting ready for my journey home I took the Princess's photograph. Before I left the king presented me with a silk purse.

"In here," he said, "is a collection of herbs from the mountains of Tibet. Keep them safe and dry and you will never ever suffer with that terrible disease of "Lumpsome back" and I never have!

"Keep your head clear and your love true until you return again to marry my daughter and be king of Tibet," he said, and he kissed me on both cheeks.

"And is she still waiting?" asked Tim. I smiled before I made answer, thinking of my own fair love Amelia.
"No Tim, I said, for when I eventually returned to Tibet the king had died of old age. The princess, as is their custom, had to marry a nobleman and he is king of Tibet even to this very day."

A Poets Tale
Frank Condon

I am Frank Condon a wandering poet,
Full of love and hope and I love to show it.
Having eyes without vision but I am that kind
I have wandered far leaving friends behind.

Going East then West I followed the sun
Writing and singing 'till my life's run.
With weary heart I wander slowly,
Like a beggar man my heart is lowly.

I wander each day towards my journey's end,
Weak and weary with neither pet nor friend.
Look at me now my back to the wall,
Playing my mouth organ for nothing at all.

With hopeless eyes sat in dark eye sockets,
Stood playing to folk with empty pockets.
I'll return age-d when my last song is sung
To the place I was born there I'll be once again young.

Register Or

Frank Condon

December was the month now the date the thirty first
On that date all emigrant Irish will surely have it cursed.
'Twas that date in eighty seven remember well the year
When the now famous Mrs. Thatcher filled all emigrant hearts with fear.

"You must register and be British or leave this counterie'
And if you don't", she pondered, "Well, just you wait and see."

The Irish have more problems than other races do
In pubs and clubs the cry was heard, 'Oh dear what shall we all do?"
No matter where you wandered or information sought,
"Sign now or be branded an Alien," there were plenty of food for thought.

The Citizens Advice Bureau were deluged by our pleas
The Solicitors too were kept busy with our extra flood of fees.
The pace had suddenly quickened an increase to sixty pounds
But after the thirty-first had past more money must be found.

One hundred and seventy pounds now, fees had increased in size,
We are paying very dearly now for our laughing Irish Eyes!!

Rememberance in London of the fallen Irish.
Frank Condon

Side by side we stood on Horseguards square.
The men from ONET and from elsewhere.
A small band of men from Eireann's Isle
Who served their country with a smile.

Through the harsh ould times as war raged on
Men died and suffered some now passed gone
But for rememberence one day each year
we set aside to parade and revere.

A day to gather, bow heads and pray
and fondly remember those passed away.
Who gave their all some only boys
That we might live in peace and enjoy.

But the men from ONET will never forget
The passing of those without regret
Whatever little we do to day
for those brave men we can never repay.

So let us remember our dead with pride
as we stand together by the Cenotaph's side
For we all lost relatives in **our** country's fight
When they too fought to set things right.

Roger the Lodger a poem
Frank Condon

Oh Mother I think I am falling
For the young man who's renting our room!
Oh please daughter don't be silly
For that lad is marrying soon.
The young man said that are you sure mom
And he is vacating his room?
The lad told me that last Tuesday
He's to marry this Saturday at noon.

Did he say where he is to marry?
In a church with a stately affair?
I don't ask questions like that pet,
To our lodger who's living upstairs.
Do you think you could ask him again mum?
 Where he is going to wed?
For it would be of interest to us mum
For he may not be right in the head.

I won't ask that man any question
As he will be leaving here soon
Well it may be too late on Saturday
If he's to be married at noon?
I don't understand your interest,
It's not very nice for a young lady

Forget all that rubbish for once mum
You see I'm expecting a baby.
But who is the father dear daughter?
And are you having it soon
I hope I don't have it 'till Saturday mum
For I'm to be married at noon.

Saint Stephen's Cemetery
Frank Condon

Saint Stephen's Cemetery is not a lonely place, for there throughout the day
Folks they come to visit, and some, to kneel and pray.
And in it's midst a stone built church, the centre point of all
An imposing entrance leads one in, and its guardian is a wall.

Is the wall put there to keep souls in? I doubt if that is so,
For all the folk that's resting there, from labours long ago
And why then is a wall put there? To keep all noise at bay?
To give this place an air of quiet, while visitors kneel to pray?

This place to me is special, for resting 'neath each sod
Are dear friends and relations that, surely rest with God?
Near that little hallowed church is, where my parents lay
I should visit there more often, if only to kneel and pray

A granddad too and a young nephew, lay sleeping here below
How sad it was at his tender years, God called he had to go
A new comer to this place of rest, though sudden and severe
Is the husband of my sister, called at Eastertide of year?

How sad it is to see each name, on tombstones high and low

My friends are numbered many here, in plots and numbered row
How sad it is to see tall grass, on forgotten burial places
How sorry I am remembering, for I can't recall their faces

I stand alone in reverie, I an old man standing here
I try so hard to be cheerful, when down my face a tear
My eyes are brimming over, it's time for me say
I go but I'll return again, if only an Ave to pray.

A CHILD IN A HOSPITAL WARD AT NIGHT
FRANK CONDON

The night was dark the lights were dim
Should have left the house but I stayed in.
The reason why I must confess
I have little knowledge but I can guess!

You see I know I'm afraid at night
Because as a child in hospital I got a fright
In a hospital ward I was all alone
Missing my family far from home

That night was windy such a gale
A big tree crashed down I felt so frail
Would the windows hold out that windy dark?
That threatened me with rain so stark

Then a ghost passed by all shimmering white
Outside my window that dark cold night
I called aloud but the ghost returned
Glowing so brightly how my eyes burnt.

Then another ghost came into sight
It too from head to toe in white?
My poor little heart was beating fast

If there were others, then the lightening flashed
The softest voice called my name quite near
In came the nurse now for me no fear.

Soldiering

Frank Condon

In the Curragh camp in fifty two
I joined the army for something to do.
In the Curragh Camp in County Kildare
I did my soldiering on Mc Donagh square.

They taught me to dress so very neat
How to deal with blisters on size 11 feet
To ate all I was given and nothing lave
It was here to that I had my very first shave.

The curse of my life with razor in hand
Cutting lumps off me face 'till they said 'that's grand'.
In the Curragh Camp in County Kildare
I spent two long years a soldiering there.

Now poor Ceannt has gone down hill.
How clean I kept it I remember still.
When I white washed stones all around that square,
Plucked tiny weeds under the sergeant's stare.

Running up and down like a high port slave,
And all because I forgot to shave.
Every single weed I plucked it out

If I didn't I hear the R S M shout.

Running up and down while defaulters blew,
To the Guardroom reporting, there was just a few.
From after tea till the bright starlight
Because by buttons weren't shining bright.

Yet another thing I must bemoan
Why was I stationed so far from home?
My mother couldn't come and spend sometimes
Help me pick up papers up and down the lines.
But I must confess I'm a defaulter slave
Each and every time when I forgot to shave.

Stoned out of my Skull.
Frank Condon.

Would you believe that my stones are still here? And you said I had nothing to fear!

With the round trip I took, I could easy write a book, you don't believe me? Well listen here.

I was calm as I left Chapeltown. I left nothing at all strewn around.

I felt no distress, in my case a nightdress, not a tear, not a fear, I was sound.

The morning was bright, the sun spread it's light, as I walked to the door in me frock.

To reception I went, you know my intent, but 'twas there that I got my first shock.

"You're not booked in here, I am sorry my dear, you must go back and see your G.P."

Well I stood my ground, as I looked all around, was this lady talking to me?

She <u>was</u> talking to me, for 'twas clear I could see, she was pointing her finger I declare!

I was tempted to cry, I guess you know why, but I just made my way towards a chair.

Then I thought I'd be bold, "Why wasn't I told?" it was a good question no lie.

She just rubbed her hands, while I watched the sands, of the time and my life passing by.

To me it was clear, so I said, "Now my dear, will we just give it give it one more go?"

"Go back home," she said, "we haven't a bed, maybe another time when we're slow."

Well I didn't like that, I wasn't here for a chat, and once again I thought I would try.

"There is nothing to give, so go home and live," then she left me as we said goodbye.

I was now all alone, so I started to roam, towards the surgery to see my G.P.

But before I got there, I was feeling right *quare,* so I toddled off home for some tea.

The Doc he knew nothing at all, "Not to worry," said he,

"sure their small.

Take a holiday or two, yes that's what you'll do, but please don't drive me up the wall!"

The Condons.
Frank Condon

A man all alone without a house or home went looking for a wife

Then he wed me maw, the first girl he saw, freed from a single life.

After six years wed, sharing a double bed, the children came along.

First came a son, a little one, though the mother done nothing wrong.

John was small in size, so he was baptised, in a county Wexford town

On Jones's hill, they remember him still, for he cried and cried and cried.

In a year or so, as John did grow, the family moved to Tinakelly
They settled down, not far from town, then a second child, that's Billy.

Two years or more, then up went the score, as Billy he grew quite lanky.
In the summer heat, she did repeat, yet another son, that's Frankie.
Didn't stop at that, for yet another chap, as two more years slipped by
A way to stop, this terrible lot, 'twas Noel that made her sigh.

Two Christmas's more, a daughter she bore, a girl by the name of Ann

When really up tight, she swore each night, that nothing had gone to plan.

She'd have no more, to her husband swore, and she never ever did

As the children grew, her husband knew, they'd never have another kid.

The kids grew big, indeed they did, the family moved back into Ross

To a rented room, where all was gloom, but mother was still the boss.

Maw was not content to pay the rent for accommodation that was small

To the council wrote and then she spoke 'twas driving her up the wall.

Just give us time, the council did chime, but they kinda liked her face
A week no more, came the key of the door, number four Haughton Place.
Settled at last we forgot the past and our school days came to an end,
We did not shirk our search for work, in our daily search she did send

A factory job, just fifteen bob, I worked 'till six each night
And Billy the same, there was no shame, the future was looking bright.

Now John did work, he did not shirk, in a Tannery making leather

"twas a grimy place, where men aged in face, no matter what the weather.

Then times were good, just as they should, then work it stopped alamed me?

To the barracks we went, we were not sent, to Join the Irish army.

All four at that, the sons of Pat, we left our home behind us.

Through the night we sped, missing a warm bed in a creaking army bus.

To join the ranks, where bullies and cranks, let no one please remind me.

What had we done, this was no fun I'm lost they'll never find me?

At bugle call, we'd gallop all, from hot beds all around

To keep in step, I'll never forget, on a perishing parade ground.

Then came the day, we were marched away, this wasn't in the book?

We had the runs, the three Condon sons, having our picture took.

As you know bye and bye, the reasons why, our picture it indorses?

To get young lads not just under Grads' to enlist in the Irish Forces.

We had had gone alone far from our home, in search for that croc-of-gold.

Some brothers went high and some went low then round in circles we never told.

For in our town if we had looked around all the things we sought were there.

We could have found a wife avoided all strife and lived without a care.

Now sister Ann she met a man, although he wasn't a local,

He was quite bold for so I'm told, he was quite but never vocal.

She didn't move far, from her maw and paw because she might be needed,

She wasn't a nurse but a daughter first, mother's words she always heeded.

Her name did change when all was arranged, married a man named Foley
She had two kids she really did he wasn't a slow man-be-the-holy.
She changed her name 'twas the husband's blame known as Foley from then on,
To our family's gain then she's still the same, though no longer known as Condon

But still and all I must recall, I've a wife that loves me still,
We've a cosy home that'll stop me roam, that will do me then until.

The children's grown we are left alone, miles from the city of London.

But, life's complete, I've a wife so sweet, who's taken my name, that's CONDON.

The Irish Club Float
Frank Condon

We had heard nothing about it, 'twas now the middle of May
And everything in the Irish Club was quietly going its way.
But then one night 'twas dropped on us sure we didn't have a hope
Says Mattie to all and sundry 'We'll enter an Irish club float'

Of what now are you talking about folks were heard to say?
'It's to do with the Lord Mayors parade bold Mattie would have his day.
Well, the club was in a turmoil *It simply can't be done*

But we had underestimated, the now famous Mattie Flynn

Mattie.

For he had got it all sussed out and in his usual way

Naturally everyone was delighted at what they saw on that day.

Now helping hands weren't plenty and with very little time

That float was put together and everything went fine.

In the middle saw our 'Irish Rose' all Regal on her throne

The float was packed with people so, she wasn't on her own.

The news boys took the corners and as they shouted out

The dancers and musicians enjoyed themselves no doubt

The famous 'Claddagh Players' were dressed as though in part
Ah the sight and sounds coming from the float gladdened every Irish heart.
Each club group was represented and were on the float that day
No doubt they'd all remember that thirty-first of May.

The judges then they made their rounds and when they came to us
With music songs and dances we raised a hell of a fuss.
Our float it rang with laughter and we really opened their eyes
But little did ever think we would ever win a prize.

Sure After that we settled down and waited for to get
Instructions for the parade to move and what's this a big rosette?
Our float had become famous and we were all surprised
When the judges in their wisdom had awarded us first prize.

Next year please god, just wait and see we'll do it all over again
When our club faces Mattie's challenge and we'll answer it like men.
Our Ladies too they will respond and answer too with pride
When we'll show them all both short and tall we're together side by side.

The Man from Ballytarsna.
Frank condon.

THE MAN FROM BALLYTARSNA.

That man from Ballytarsna arrived in Swindon Town,

Looking for work as we'd all done on building sites around.

His foxy hair and body lean showed no lack of skill,

Then settled down in Wavell Road staying there until,

He started on a building site 'twas there he earned his pay'

To pay his digs and save a bit to cover his wedding day.

Did I tell you he had a girl friend? A girl from near his home

He was not like us at all, at all, that came to England on their own.

Michael worked with me and done his bit through rain and hail and sleet

We built the British Home Stores, now standing in Regent's Street.

Stripped to the waist we whistled at girls, some they whistled back

Ah those were the days on the buildings, hard work but plenty of craic.

That man from Ballytarsna he married his true love,

In the chapel of Holy Rood as the sun shone from above.

We all went to the party a sit down meal no less

The lads all wished him well that day, they wanted to I guess.

But Michael was sad and lonely for his homeland far away
They both decided that England was not their place to stay.
So Margaret Ann and Michael worked hard and saved their pay
While saving they'd make plans for a return home some day

A man is dead and gone now who lived in New Ross Town,
he came from Ballytarsna his likes will ne'er be found.
His Cherie voice of welcome as he opened wide the door,
"Hello, how are you, please come in," we'll never hear no more.
A big red face, the foxy hair what a memory they'd create,
yes, that man from Ballytarsna he really was a trate.

He travelled far he travelled wide, even China he was there,

his job though very tedious the wages they were fair.

For those who suffered a grievous loss, his sympathy he's extending,

for love and understanding he dispensed right to his ending.

He helped the poor afflicted who suffered some terrible fate,

yes, that man from Ballytarsna you'll find him hard to bate.

He toiled to build a family home, out there in far Knockmullen,

he worked in cold, he worked in rain he worked in weather sullen.

Slowly that little family home rose up e'en block on block,

the ground was good the ground was sound he'd built his home on rock.

He worked from early morning and until the hour was late,

yes that man from Ballytarsna he's never yet been bate.

He raised a family took a wife and built a home so sound,

he had a bit of help though for a solid wife he'd found.

They built a little business, at first though it was slack,

but anyone who stayed there always wanted to come back.

Yes, everyone enjoyed their stay they were even glad they stayed,

yes that man from Ballytarsna at last he'd got it made.

Well, they lived happy ever after that family of four,

a husband, wife, a daughter and son who could ask for more.

His wife is now quite famous, as is the daughter and son,

that man named Michael Foley a real good job had done.

But then the Lord he called poor Michael high up to heaven's gate,

yes, that man from Ballytarsna is now rewarded for his faith.

He went to mass Ash Wednesday for that bless-ed ashes sign,

his wife, she walked behind him and everything was fine.

While sat at home in his favourite chair he quietly slipped away

 and troubled no one as he died on that bless-ed ashes day.

He had to go for he'd been called for sure he couldn't be late

for that man from Ballytarsna with saint Peter had a date.

That man is gone but still linger on memories of that man that came to town, his smiling face around the place he was never known to frown.

His ready hand in friendship grand, begrudged it never was and he gave his all to large and small he was just like that because.

He hailed from Ballytarsna and came looking for a mate and found instead a home and bed a good cook and plenty to ate.

Though sadly missed his life was blest as seen in the way he died, though tears may flow that he can never more go by Ballytarsna side.

Instead we know as the years may go while looking from above, for his family dear may have no fear, for he's looking down with love

"The New Ross Standard."
Frank Condon

I have roamed the whole world over yes I have really been around but nowhere in this big wide world, nicer place have found.

Than my birthplace in Co. Wexford and the town of Ros Mhic Treoin where I left so many years ago to seek my fortune all alone.

I left behind my parents who had been very good to me my hers and sister also no longer would I see.

For times were hard and work was scarce and so I had to leave I would return one day I thought, this I honestly did believe.

The time soon passed I took a wife and then came a family my thoughts of home grew less and less and almost ceased to be.
Until one day the post arrived and "The Standard," the lord be praised then over the years and many miles came memories through the haze.

I would read about the folk's back home and of people I had never seen I would read about the shops and streets and the places I had once been.

Oh how the years would fall away and I'd be a lad once more where I did sport and play as on many a day all along that River Barrow shore.

So for many years the "Standard" has brought my home to me I could read of what's going on there and the changes that's going to be.
I can read of who's got married and who's taken a new wife of childer born to Pat and Mike and who's departed this life.

The price of pigs and cattle or who has hay for sale and who has reached the big nine oh and is still pulling the divil by the tail.

So it's thanks then to "The New Ross Standard" that I won't be too far from home from my birthplace in Co. Wexford and the town of "Ros Mhic Treoin."

The play that never was.
Frank Condon.

The crowd was very little in the club that Saturday night so a

crowd of us got thinking that we'd soon put that to right.

We couldn't all do magic, nor could we ever stoop to do

what other groups do so we formed a drama troupe.

So the drama group was started and 'twas clearer every day

that we could start rehearsals if we only had a play!

We hunted through the libraries to find a goodly tale we

would start with something decent we didn't want to fail.

When we eventually got a script and we thought that it was

fair it was on the television called "Sailor beware."

And so we practised every night and we bought videotape and as the weeks turned into months it started to take shape. Now nine was numbered in the cast and though we never allowed that with more than three people that is indeed a crowd.

At first one weren't well at all then two more it affected their head two more took off for China when they should have stayed home instead.

Now as the time was marching on for us it would not stay for those that were left behind at the club rehearsed and read the play.

Now some were reading two parts and some were reading four 'till eventually thing got so bad we couldn't take no more.

Eventually after all this time when everyone one got cross

we produced the best we ever did the play that never was!

The Show would go to Middlewood?
Frank Condon.

The show would go to "Middlewood," of that there was no doubt, if only to find our failings then we could iron them out.

We didn't expect any problems, up to then we'd missed no line our confidence was very high and every thing would be fine.

So at the club while waiting, we'd rehearse our play once more until the sounds of transport was heard outside the door.

We rehearsed our way to "Middlewood," there really was no fuss, we all sat amongst our props and things while "Matty," drove the bus.

When we got to the theatre, "Matty," had us there within a tick, we unloaded all our scenery and got costumed very quick.

The stage was set already that did save us some time positions please and curtain, still every thing was fine.

The lines they started going wrong the director paced about, then came that crucial moment and the lights they never went out!

Now where the hell is Martin? We cannot find the door they will surely throw us out now and let us back no more.

The curtain dropped to save us all to end that one act play, but our "problems" if you could call them that, just did not go away.

The variety acts were chaos, the costumes were all wrong, with flea acts and mind readers, going on half way through a song.

Now some were dressed to do their act, to do their very best, to give a good impression and be better than the rest.

"It's time for bed then," someone said, "we'll end the show right here," I'm not ready for the finale, oh dear, oh dear, oh dear.

The panic in both dressing rooms I'd end it if I could, but we'll never forget that night, we took our show to "Middlewood."

Three Rings
Frank Condon

A wise man once told me that behind every door,

There is a cross or two or even more.

However, going through life you will meet many things.

So, let me tell you about life's three rings.

You will meet boy or girl and you will want to shout.

Your eyes will shine as you start to walk out.

You will share your love and everything.

If the answer is "yes" there is your very first **Ring.**

Engaged to the loveliest person in town.

You have looked but none that is nicer you have found.

Enjoy your life let love take wing.

The joys of love then a wedding **Ring.**

Then off through life with a family.

First one then two then maybe three.

The family grows as the years they flew.

They marry, they are gone, then it's only us two.

Then comes a time when one slips away.

You never thought life could end this way.

Now comes the time for that very last ring.

When life is full of pain and suffeRing.

Look past this time when you are all alone.

We will all meet again when God calls us home.

Frank Condon.

The Travelling Bachelor.
Frank Condon.

I was a rover whose heart wanted to roam; I had eyes with no vision and a heart with no home.

Far have I wandered but no happiness found, now I'm left with only memories of places around.

My travels have robbed me of a youth I misspent, my heart it is broken I've no money for rent.

There is only one place left on the ladders last rung, in the midst of my people where I'd be once again young.

I have eyes without vision and my heart has no home, I have long been a rover with a yearning to roam.

Far have I wandered in searching for what? now I'm left with only memories that is all that I've got.

My memories have robbed me of a life thrown away, my clothes are all wrinkled from nights spent in the hay.

I have given much thought now to why I am this way, but nothing makes sense now at the end of my day.

'Tis time I returned now to where my heart will find home, I have spent too long in sadness in misery and alone.

So let the journey commence never mind what I've done, I am heading for home where I'll be once again young.

I am heading at speed for that place I love best, back to my home place where I can lay down and rest.

With the cold earth below me and above me as well, no words on my tombstone for there's nothing to tell.

Twas Love I was after.
Frank Condon.

'Twas in Priory Street in her two bare feet, I saw her first that day.

Her foxy hair blew everywhere, 'twas a windy month that May.

She wasn't a flirt but her flowery skirt, blew high above her knee

What a sight I guess when that flowery dress, a view was offered me.

A milk white thigh I could see so high, a paradise I view

There's no reason why I could but try, to get together us two.

Now Breda Malone lived near my home, a beauty I'd never seen.

Such beauty and grace set my heart to race, where on earth had I been?

She was so nice; I've seen her since twice and each time it seemed like a dream.

Such beauty a fair at my heart did tear; she was surely a beauty queen.

I spoke to day as she passed my way, but her eyes never strayed towards me,

To tell it so takes my heart so low, what's the matter with me?

My kindly smile might hold her a while, but still she did not stay.

I must seek another as told by my brother, in this windy month of May.

'Twas the month of June and very soon, I was back in love once more.
'Twas with Molly Breen with eyes so green, that I saw on the sandy shore.
'Twas in a fog as she walked her dog, in the early morning mist.
She passed me by and she winked her eye, she was different from the rest.

At the rusty school gate and I was late, she came running up to me.

But passing me by I winked my eye, for she too was late you see.

I'd said nothing wrong but she just walked on, and Molly was gone from me.

No never no more on that sandy shore, would I ever go near the sea.

I looked at the blue sky with a tear in my eye, hoping something would happen soon.

But I'd left it late by the old school gate, and that was the end of June.

'Twas in July 'neath a clear blue sky, A Colleen I chanced to meet

At her auburn hair I was drawn to stare and she had shoes on her feet.

To see her lovely smile I'd walk a mile she was about my height as well.

With personables like these I was so pleased, I was in love and I could tell.

Her pleasant voice gave me no choice, she knew I was impressed

When she shook her head sure I nearly dropped dead, was she putting me to the test?

I did entreat it was some feat, 'till an impish gleam in her eye,

What can I say we were married next May to the girl that I met in July?

Unwanted Gift.
Frank Condon

The unasked for gift arrived to day.

It was puzzling?

The grieving for a mother figure perhaps?

In her stead a pale waxen image.

Disease river flesh shorn from bones now covered with thin skin.

Leaving nothing but a wan emaciated body.

Useless vision covered by closed lids.

Lank hair covers soundless ears.

Whispered prayers go unheard,

Mourners stand helpless in the presence of death.

What a useless gift is death?

Sought by few, unwanted by most.

And yet it was welcomed by the family for Mum's sake.

Us Irish
Frank Condon

A funny old lot is us Irish, we struggle through strife and hard times
We work at a task, and we hope it won't last, hopefully then we'll be fine.
I remember a time, when all was not fine and we had a club we could meet
But 'twasn't for long, 'cause it all went wrong, and now we're out walking the street.

How sad it was, and all because, well, yeh know we never complain
There was plenty of proof, we'd a leaky roof that didn't keep out the rain.
That Irish club, well it was the hub, for drama music and dance.
There was no man, like John Dowling can, play a tune when given the chance.

Now Tommy Lynch could sing like a finch or any of t'other birds
He could sing all night, sometimes getting it right, if only he'd remember the words.

Oh he was good at the quiz, he knew his biz, and some answers they were tatty
But best of all in that Irish hall was the genius known as Mattie.

That man was good but never rude, there were things over which he could gloat,
Like on many a time when the weather was fine he put us all on a Lord Mayor's Float.
He didn't leave it at that, he took round a hat collecting all he could get.
For the money he raised, he was oft times praised, and we won a first place rosette.

For meself sure I planned Irish Plays oh so grand, which filled people up with delight.
Seen on stage every time, while remembering line, for a pound they'd a wonderful night.
From all round they came, in the dark and the rain,, to watch to listen and see
For our gang one and all, entertained big and small, while I was as proud as can be.

A short one act play, the lines we would say, and songs they'd heard oft before
They'd heard of our fame and that's why they came, coming excitedly thru the door.
Ah those were the time, when been Irish was fine, as we gathered together each night,

Having too much to drink, well what do you think there was always a bit of fright.

Spring Summer and Fall we enjoyed it all, as we neared the end of an era,
Now every Sunday, which should be a fun-day, there's sad faces of Pat, Mick and Vera.
T'old club it is gone, memories still linger on, when the craic was solid and sound,
There were none that could see, it wasn't cost free, and that's why were walking around.

WAS IT ALL A DREAM?
Frank Condon.

While under the anaesthetic in dream like state I wander, while up above a surgeon works cutting my flesh asunder?

In total silence here I sleep without a care or woe I could leave my body and wander but where on earth to go?

The long, long wait is over I finally got a bed, the operation would soon be over, so the Surgeon said.

What's this a long long tunnel and a light ahead I see, no darkness here, just a clear white light that doesn't frighten me.

I walk the well-lit pathway, the soft light like the moon, to reach the end I hurry I would reach it very soon.

I walk for what seemed ages, for I know I can't delay, am I on some sort of conveyor belt that's travelling the other way?

My quest is getting harder for I cannot reach the light, I run I gallop in stages but the end is still not in sight.

I know that when I get there it will be a land all bright the entrance to this special place must be that shining light.

I hear some one calling me in front or far behind? I will not answer their calling until this lovely land I've found.

The tunnel it is fading, will I miss my chance to see, the land at the end of the tunnel, someone still calls out to me?

"Wake up, wake up," the voice it calls, with urgency ringing through, "Your operation's over dear, can you hear me calling you."

Where is Peace?
Frank Condon.

From early morning to sunset bright,
 we wake each morning to see daylight.
Without a worry, without a care?
Where are you living, please tell me where?

In another world quite far away?
For here we see a different day.
A world of terror, a world of fright,
we see it hear it from morn 'till night.

It's on the tele' in the papers too
 we simply do not know what to do!
It's very scary I have to say
 whether you're old or just one day.

Sometimes it's in a far off land
other times it's really close at hand,
So tell me, where's this wonderful place
where each one person is blessed with peace?

Where war and weapons are used no more,

how I'd like to walk on that peaceful shore.
Maybe your fibbing, is there such a spot?
I need to know this is not a plot.

Just speak its name, no it can't be true
that's not a place for me or you!
Lead on then friend as though I'm blind
and let all humanity walk behind.

This is a cemetery, please stop or cease,
is it here where you promised we'd all have peace?
Surely there must be something else to say
 what of love and peace, we tried that all of our yesterdays.

Where the River Barrow flows.
AIR—(*where the river Shannon flows*)
Frank Condon.

Cross the briny ocean he is goin
To where the wheat and barley is growin
To where the scented winds are blowin
To where the River Barrow flows.

There's a colleen there that's waitin
At a farm gate there's Kate'n
Who knows she is not forsaken
Where the River Barrow flows.

When a day 'ere comes to pass
When he'll return again to Ross
A wide ocean he must cross
To where the River Barrow flows

When the spring skies they are starry
He'll be aheadin home to marry
That ship's captain he must hurry
To where the River Barrow flows

Arriving on the quay side
Kate will rush to be his spring bride

But he just lasted 'till the next tide
Where the River Barrow flows

There 's no need to be awailin
Just because his health was failin
It's his fault for emigratin
Slowly--From where the River Barrow flows.

Young Nancy.
Frank Condon.

That night was dark when she left me, that silly young bitch of mine.

When last I saw her she was running, heading straight for the lights of town.

We never fell out though we never talked much and now she's up and gone.

I racked my brains by the fire each night, was it something I did wrong?

We worked together on the land all day without a word been said.

Maybe if I had spoken more, now I'd rest easier in my bed.

Should I get up and follow her, maybe bring her back by the ear?

Maybe I should but I didn't perhaps it was out of fear.

Fear that she might not come with me in the dark of a winter's night,

Fear that if she walked home with me she would miss the city lights.

What if she'd been enticed away, away from the toil and muck?

By something wearing a flashy coat and that's about my luck.

For what had I to offer, hard work and then little pay.

A place to rest from the cold of night and the smell of new mown hay?
But Nancy wasn't one to be enticed away from the land we loved so well,
Nor was she one that would turn her back, well she wasn't I could tell.

In the heat of the day we would curl up in the shade of the Coolibar tree,
With a blue sky above and no cloud to be seen 'twas a wonderful place to be.
But now she's gone and I sit here alone, alone like a lonely bullfrog.
I'll remember the day that she went away for she was a hard working dog.

Elina Alina
Frank Condon

They walked down the boreen just him and Eileen
He wheeled his bike they were going to mass.
The sunlight was shining, young Eileen beguiling
And not even a soul did they pass.

Now Michael, says she, will you listen to me?
I'm leaving, I'm going away.
You leaving', says he, what will happen to me?
If you're going I cannot stay?

You'll find someone else, I can't be left on the shelf,
because me poor mother did say.
For seven long years you've been courting I fear,
He'll not ask you to marry, so why should you tarry,
You're pathway is very unclear.

I've no job nor no money, so have patience honey,
How is it that you cannot see?
I'd marry tomorrow and then you'd be sorry
Because you see I'm not free.

Your married you say, why tell me to day?
I'd have said so before but I cannot say more
You are the best part of my life
But I'll always love you, I'm crazy about you

And one day I'll make you my wife.

Sure how can that be? Oh why didn't I see?
A fine man like yourself would be wed!
I see you're upset but I cannot forget
my wife, whose only seven years dead!

I have no a body to day.
Frank Condon

At seven years old I done well at school

I fell over regularly and felt a fool

But that hurt it healed and come what may

But kindly look at the body I have to day?

At twenty the girls took advantage of me

Dragged me down the lanes and all for free

They used me cruelly without any pay

but look at this body I have to day.

At thirty I wasn't the same man at all

When I stood up, I looked quite tall

I perished in winter, summer made the hay

but look at the body I have to day

At ninety one I still felt strong

But feeble with age now can't go on

I died that year so what can I say

It's no wonder I haven't a body but clay

SELF INFLICTED
Frank Condon

Now words got round when it was found when the Enterprise last came.

Our folks were pleased that our troubles ceased 'cause they had stopped our rain.

Our terrible plight it was a fright that rains not stopped for years,

We couldn't fly, though we did try, their coming eased our fears.

Then word got out, speak soft don't shout, for it really is fantastic

For it was said, earthling were easily led, for their all-accepting **plastic.**

Now plans were made, 'fore our six suns did fade, for a journey to that planet

Our ships were good, we used no wood, the earth was there so scan it.

A thousand ships, made up of bits, were sent hurtling through the air

The fat, the tall, the kids and all, for 'twas to be a great affair.

From beginning to end our spacecraft did bend, around each asteroid belt.

'Twas quicker that way, or so they say, that's how the elders felt.

Our budget spent, 'twas borrowed and lent, our money stretched like 'elastic.

'Cause in our head, were the words that were said, the Earthling's dealt in plastic.

As on we onward sped, even our double bed, we'd melted down for wealth
Our garage too, our car 'twas new, we'd be covered by national health
Our spacecrafts were made, of the finest grade, we'd worked so hard to get.
There was thermogloss, and chemosloss, that stuff's very hard to set
In colours blue, to a greenish hue, which were held together by mastic
As we earthwards bound, with joyous sound, just to spend our plastic.

Show business (amateur)
Frank Condon.

Just two nights a week and our pay is your smile please join us on show night if just for a while.

When we're standing up here with our head in the clouds when the people's applauding and the roar of the crowds.

The excitement is heady in the glare of the lights it's a wonderful way to fill cold winter's nights.

We've no pay I'm afraid but we are glad to take part so don't shed a tear for we've fun in our heart.

See the face of that child watch the gleam in their eye as the show it unfolds they can't hide their surprise.

The old folks have all come not to be on their own fill them up with laughter and some to take home.

Now I hope I have given you a little insight what it's like to be standing this side the footlights.

So on with the show but do spare a thought for the cast here tonight and the pleasure they brought.

Long after the lights out and the hall it is quiet old folks will remember your sounds and your sights.

The Ballad of Butler's Hill.
Frank Condon

Oh people well remember the battle of Butler's Hill,

No shot was ever fired there and probably never will.

The cause of all the trouble, 'twas well known to one and all.,

The Mooneys they were fighting and never stopped at all.

A policeman from the village, who never heard of Butler's Hill,

Was sent to stop the fighting that went on up on the hill.

He pulled out his truncheon and gave a whistle blow,

Which attracted all the people in the valley down below.

A bus was filled and up the hill came people by the score,
To see this brave young policeman now rapping on the door.
Mrs. Mooney wasn't fighting she was having a quiet day,
She was stokeing up the fire in preparation for the tay.

The poor woman wasn't hard of hearing she just didn't hear,

The police went behind the house he didn't show no fear.

He saw the group of men there fighting just behind the wall,

So he surrounded and arrested them, the Mooneys one and all.

He marched them down that rocky slope there really was no fuss,

But halfway down that rocky road they were run over by the bus.

The ballad of John Condon
Frank Condon

My name it is John Condon a Wexford man no more,
Born in a house on Jones's Hill I'm now aged 79.
In the family I am the eldest the family it well knew,
Head and shoulders high above them all until my brother's grew.
I headed out for England in the year of forty-nine
To work upon the railway, as a fireman I'd be fine,
They sent me here they sent me there and I never was a boss
'Till I drew my pay one summer's day, and headed back to Ross.

In Ross I stated working indeed not a very nice job
Making leather in the Tanyard my wage was fifteen bob.
Again I was redundant and to the Army went
From New Ross to the Curragh Camp, well, 'twas there that I was sent
For two long years I served there, a Signalman no less

Now when ever I came to New Ross town the girls I did impress.
There is something about a uniform, I did impress the lot,
Little thinking if we went to war that I could of course get shot!

And now I've started drinking, in Kavanagh's I'll be found
Married with four childer I'll spend my days around,
The town where I was born and not even now the boss,
But my name is still John Condon, from Jones's Hill in Ross.

The little town of New Ross.
Frank Condon.

Though my memory it is fading, my thoughts oft wander still, to the little town of New Ross by the Barrow River on the hill.

I think of my dear school days when only just a boy, when I walked across to Michael Street I remember them with joy.

Our route was from the Irishtown and straight through Nunnery lane, it took us twenty minutes then though much quicker if it rained.

I remember our schoolmaster, Mr. O'Donovan was his name, he's in heaven now, God rest his soul, heavens his right to claim.

He rode across the old bridge, 'twas then three miles per hour, along the quay and up Michael Street he never seemed to tire.

Our school was all for lads then, the girl's school further down, they kept us separated in the forties in our town.
From school, I started working Driver Harris was the job and each long day from eight to six we worked for fifteen bob.
So each morn' at eight o'clock when the hooter made its sound, the boys and men and girls on bikes they came from miles around.

We'd work then 'till the hooters sound, told us 'twas twelve o'clock, we'd all rushed home 'twas dinnertime though the machinery didn't stop.
I remember too when work got slack we worked two days per week, times were very hard just then and everything looked bleak.
For quite some time we wandered but no job could be found, our little town was silent then, we missed that hooters sound.

The chance it came I took it and across the world I went but once I started wandering now I'll never be content.

Through all my years of wandering, my memory holds it still, that little town of New Ross by the River Barrow on the hill.

The Tryst.
Frank Condon.

God above I hope she's there. Who? The girl with the ringlets and nut-brown hair.

Too nice a day for wearing a suit, I'm much too warm, will she give a hoot?

Shoes off for me in a cool, cool stream, not riding a bike to a rendezvous dreams.

That is the place where I should be, down in the shade of that big beech tree.

Down by the bull rushes casting a line, now there is a place that would suit me fine.

The blooming chain on this bike's got too much oil if it gets on my slacks 'twill surely spoil.

That big brown trout by that fallen tree would make a good supper for mother and me.

The Black Knot fly will see him right then a beautiful dinner for us tonight.

I'm early I know I should slow down, why are we meeting so far from town?

That big brown trout, now there's a treat, having him for tea will upset our street.

I'm riding away from that silver stream she says she loves me, what does that mean?

Now I'm over the stream and along by the wall, what if she's not there at all?

Would I have wasted a beautiful day? If she is not there what could I say?

Now where did I put my fishing gear I only used it the one time last year.

I'm almost sure now she won't come at all, am I heading for a disastrous fall?

Ah my mother was right and she's a pearl, I'm much to young to be going out with a girl.

I'll turn and fish for my mother's tea she is the one that's been good to me.

The wedding invitation to the USA.
Frank Condon.

When the letter came that morning I just got out of bed,
to make the tea I'd come downstairs, my turn, so she said.
So I set the kettle to boil up and have a golden brew,
 set the tray with cups and things, we were having tea for two.
A letter lay upon the mat with a postmark from far away,
 a wedding invitation no less, from Boston USA.

I shouted up the stairs to her, regarding what I'd found,
 and in no time at all at all she came tumbling down.
I picked her up and sat her down, then plied her with some tea,
 then I told her all that happened but she wasn't hearing me.
The fall that my poor wife had, had bruised her bum and head,
 and so she wasn't listening to anything I said.

Her head it ached, her bum was sore but that's poor consolation,
the day we got from the USA our wedding invitation.

We checked our passports, they were okay and they hadn't expired,
sent for visas, booked our 'plane this made us very tired.
The fourth October finally came, the bus it left on time,
and Heathrow Airport by half past nine and everything was fine.
It must have been three miles of subways that lay ahead of us,
 what a place to put an aeroplane three miles from the terminus.
Especially when you're walking and at a ripe old age,
then mile after mile of subways can fill ones mind with rage.

We sat aboard a seven four seven, a very sumptuous 'plane,

weather, bright and sunny though forecasters had promised rain.

Now everything comes to him who waits and that's no easy feat,

another hour and were flying at thirty three thousand feet.

Well the 'plane droned on for hours and hours, what a terrible place to be,

nothing outside but clouds and sky below us the open sea.

They served us dinner, we ate it all and had a bottle of wine,

this really is the way to live and we are still doing fine.

They served us coffee and then lacquers sure everything was groovy,

until they asked for money, to listen to the in flight movie.

The captain he was saying, that when we get off the plane,

we better put our raincoats on because in Boston they had rain.

Well it wasn't really rain he said, more like a couple of showers,

and would we go to Boston time, turn our watches back five hours.
We are standing on American soil, there is nothing much to see,
and at six PM in Boston it's dark in the land of the free.
As we walk along the subways, they have them here as well,
is anyone here to meet us, it's late, it's hard to tell.
We proceed to baggage pickup our baggage is coming round,
the wife has gone round scouting and our driver she has found.
He grabs a case, I grab one too, he warmly welcomes us,
and then in his car we are travelling far
with six thousand miles behind us.
Out into the countryside we are brought to live amongst the trees,
it was there we spent a pleasant week, very much at our ease.
We died two days or so it seems but then we came around,
and from our bed in this big house peace it was we found.
So slowly as time passes and we waken more and more,

the autumn sun is shining through the window and the door.
So this is Massachusetts with its coloured leaves and all,
I'm glad we came to Massachusetts for it's lovely in the fall.
The sights and sounds were new to us and each and every day,
we walked through woods, on roads and paths, what a lovely place to stay.
The old friends that we met there, took us on a whirlwind tour,
to seaside spots, to shopping malls and to a forty second floor.
It's many years since that happened, though it seems like yesterday,
that we got the wedding invitation to that great big USA.